RYE FREE READING ROOM

FLOOD RELIEF 2007

Purchased with
Generous Community Support
After the Flood of 2007

Thank You!

Rosie and Buttercup

With love, for Don and Moo, for Jas and Julie,
and for Paul, as always — C.U.

To my little sister, Nathalie — S.J.

Kids Can Press acknowledges the financial support of the Government of Ontario, through the Ontario Media Development Corporation's Ontario Book Initiative; the Ontario Arts Council; the Canada Council for the Arts; and the Government of Canada, through the BPIDP, for our publishing activity.

Published in Canada by
Kids Can Press Ltd.
29 Birch Avenue
Toronto, ON M4V 1E2

Published in the U.S. by
Kids Can Press Ltd.
2250 Military Road
Tonawanda, NY 14150

www.kidscanpress.com

The artwork in this book was rendered in watercolor.
The text is set in Palatino.

Edited by Tara Walker
Designed by Karen Powers
Printed and bound in Singapore

This book is smyth sewn casebound.

CM 08 0 9 8 7 6 5 4 3 2 1

Library and Archives Canada Cataloguing in Publication

Uegaki, Chieri
   Rosie and Buttercup / written by Chieri Uegaki ; illustrated by Stéphane Jorisch.

ISBN 978-1-55337-997-3

I. Jorisch, Stéphane II. Title.

PS8591.E32R68 2008   jC813'.6   C2007-904098-5

Kids Can Press is a **LORUS**™ Entertainment company

Rosie and Buttercup

Written by Chieri Uegaki

Illustrated by Stéphane Jorisch

KIDS CAN PRESS

$\mathcal{R}osie$ was a girl who had everything.

She had dance on Wednesdays and voice on Fridays.

She had two pet crickets named Eenie and Meenie, a bag full of sun-dried dandelion puffs and a mother and father whom she loved more than anything.

Truly, whenever she had a moment, Rosie would think that she couldn't ask for anything more.

Then along came Buttercup.

When Rosie's little sister arrived, Rosie was enchanted. She wrote songs about Buttercup, one for each day of the week, and sang them to help her to sleep.

She thought it marvelous when Buttercup learned to pull off her own socks. (The sock game soon became their favorite.)

And even though Buttercup could not yet *plié*,
Rosie allowed her to join in every backyard ballet.

Unfortunately, things between the two sisters were not always so harmonious.

Sometimes, when Rosie wanted to be alone, she would put Buttercup away in the time-out tent.

Or, when no one was looking, Rosie would take Buttercup's last bit of pumpkin or drink her last sip of milk.

And when Buttercup's cries reached operatic heights, Rosie would cover her ears and muse very loudly, "Remember how quiet it *used* to be around here?"

One morning, Rosie woke up feeling peevish, and as she listened to Buttercup whistling in her sleep nearby, a tiny idea that had been smoldering in her head burst into flame. She suddenly thought to herself, "I don't *want* a baby sister."

At first, Rosie hoped the thought would go away. And perhaps all would have been fine if only Rosie hadn't caught Buttercup trying to open Eenie and Meenie's cage.

"Buttercup!" Rosie said as she grabbed the cage away. "You are not allowed to touch! These are my crickets. *My* crickets, understand? Mine."

"Mine," said Buttercup.

Rosie clenched her teeth. "No. *Mine*."

"*Mine*," said Buttercup again, and she laughed.

Rosie stomped away. "Mother," she said, "Buttercup is making me crazy."

But Mother was busy and all she said was, "Rosie, why don't you take Buttercup outside to play?"

Her mind buzzing, Rosie took Buttercup
and the crickets out into the yard. She hung
the cage in a tree and plopped Buttercup on
the grass. She stood thinking for a minute,
then put Buttercup in her stroller and started
down the sidewalk.

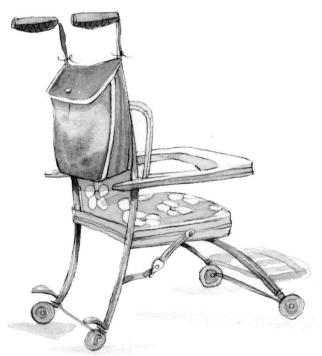

Two houses over, Rosie marched up to the front door. She
knocked a firm *tap-ta-tap-tap*. Her sitter, Oxford, answered.

"Hey, Rosie," said Oxford.

"Hi," she said, lifting Buttercup out of the stroller. "I brought you a present. Here."

"You're giving me Buttercup?"

"Yup," Rosie replied. "And for free."

Oxford raised his eyebrows. "Do your parents know about this?" he asked.

"Not exactly," said Rosie.

"I see." Oxford took Buttercup from Rosie. Buttercup smiled her brightest smile. "I see," she said, reaching for Oxford's whiskers.

Satisfied she'd found Buttercup a good home, Rosie turned to leave.

"Bye, Oxford," she said.

Buttercup clapped. "Rosie!" she called. "Ro-sie."

As she looked back at Buttercup, comfortable in Oxford's arms, Rosie felt a funny kind of squeezy feeling in her chest. She crisscrossed her arms tight to stop it.

"Wave bye-bye, Buttercup," said Oxford.

"Oxford?"

"Yes, Rosie?"

"She likes it when you sing to her. And her favorite food is pumpkin. And …"

"Don't worry," said Oxford.

"We'll be fine. And drop by anytime."

Walking away, Rosie felt strangely light,

like she'd forgotten her schoolbag on the bus.

"But this is what I wanted," she told herself. "Things back to the way they used to be — just Mother, Father and me."

Rosie started to skip down the sidewalk. (Skipping always made her feel better.) And by the time she was home, all Rosie could think about was how nice and big and empty the house would feel without Buttercup. "No more crying, no more shushing, no more sharing *everything*."

As she took Eenie and Meenie
down from the tree, she blew them each
a kiss. "You're safe now," she said and ran to her room.

There, Rosie took a bag of dandelion puffs from under her bed, popped a
puff into her mouth and settled down to bask in the feeling of having
everything all to herself once more.

That soon grew boring.

So Rosie put tethers on Eenie and Meenie and tried to teach them to hop through hoops.

Then she worked on a routine for a one-rodent revue she dreamed of performing one day.

But eventually that, too, lost its appeal.

Searching for something else to do, Rosie surveyed the room ("*My* room," she reminded herself) and felt surprised by all the Buttercup-stuff that was there.

As she noticed the hint of talcum powder in the air, the toys strewn like acorns on the floor and the silly socks Buttercup never liked to wear on the dresser, Rosie realized an astonishing thing.

She missed her little sister.

She picked up a photo of her family. There they were, Rosie on her father's knee, Buttercup on her mother's. Rosie covered one eye with her hand and tried to block Buttercup out of the picture, but it didn't work.

Rosie put the photo down. The funny squeezy feeling in her chest came back. She looked at Eenie and Meenie and sighed. "I'm sorry, boys," she said.

A short while later, Rosie was back knocking on Oxford's door.

"Hey, Rosie," said Oxford. "Nice pillowcase."

"I'm here to make a trade," Rosie said. "For Buttercup."

"Oh, really?"

Rosie reached into the pillowcase. "Here," she said, pulling out her bag of sun-dried dandelion puffs. "I only ate five."

"Well, I do love a good dandelion puff …" said Oxford.

"And these," Rosie continued. She held up her cage and chirps filled the room. She heard Buttercup chirping back.

"Eenie and Meenie?" said Oxford.

"That's a fair trade, isn't it?" said Rosie.

"I'll say. All this for one sister?"

Rosie nodded.

Oxford weighed the dandelion puffs in his hand. He peered at the crickets. "I don't know," he said. "We've been having a pretty good time together."

Rosie's heart jumped like a poked frog. What if puffs and crickets weren't enough? She had brought nothing more. She crossed her fingers and held her breath.

"Tell you what, Rosie," Oxford said finally. "I'm allergic to crickets, so you keep Eenie and Meenie. But fair's fair, so I'll keep the puffs and you can take Buttercup. Deal?"

Rosie grinned. "Deal," she said.

Back in their yard, Rosie took center stage.

"Now pay attention, Buttercup," said
Rosie. She pointed to Eenie. "This one
is mine, okay? M-i-n-e, mine." She pointed
to Meenie. "That one," she said, "I'll give
you, okay? *That* one is yours."

"Yours," said Buttercup.

"No, *yours*."

"*Yours*." Buttercup laughed and
rolled over on the warm grass.

"You're a funny girl, Buttercup,"
Rosie said, shaking her head.

But she laughed, too. And then, with
a great deal of pomp, Rosie premiered
her soon-to-be famous cricket act, much
to Buttercup's delight.

JP   Uegaki, Chieri.

            Rosie and Buttercup.